VOLUME I

HOW TO MANAGE
CONFLICT
IN THE CHURCH
UNDERSTANDING & MANAGING CONFLICT

HOW TO MANAGE CONFLICT IN THE CHURCH:
Understanding and Managing Conflict

Copyright © 1983 by
Norman Shawchuck, Ph.D

Printed in the United States of America
Sixth Printing 1998

Published by:

SPIRITUAL GROWTH RESOURCES®
Telephone: 1•800•359•7363

ISBN 0-938180-10-X

MANUAL CONTENTS

Lord, make me an instrument of thy peace.
Where there is hatred,
let me sow love.
Where there is resentment,
let me bring forgiveness.
Where there is discord,
let me bring harmony.
Where there is error,
let me bring truth.
Where there is doubt,
let me bring faith.
Where there is despair,
let me bring hope.
Where there is darkness,
let me bring joy.
Guide me that I may not
so much seek to be consoled
as to console,
to be understood
as to understand,
to be loved as to love.
For it is in giving
that we receive,
in forgetting ourselves
that we find ourselves,
in forgiving that we are forgiven.
And it is in dying
that we are born to eternal life.

— ST. FRANCIS OF ASSISI

Gaining Self-Awareness of the Way you Think and Act in Conflict — and Why You Act That Way

In this section you will:

STEP 1: Develop a Biblical Understanding of Conflict

STEP 2: Develop an Understanding of Your Behavior
in Conflict Situations

STEP 3: Develop an Understanding of Each
Conflict Management Style

STEP 4: Discover the Basic Concerns Which
Determine Your Conflict
Management Style

SECTION I
GAINING SELF-AWARENESS

Step 1

Develop a Biblical Understanding of Conflict

A unique characteristic of the church is that it is the world's greatest agent for peace — yet its very message is conflict producing.

Jesus, the Prince of Peace, said, "I have not come to bring peace, but a sword." When the church is at its very best in terms of faithful living and preaching, it is then its conflicts may be greatest in number and intensity.

What does God think about this? What does He actually think about conflict in the church? Finding the answer to this question is our place of beginning . . .

The church is a theological being, and its theology influences what it does and how it does it. The church's theology guides its selection of the materials and methods it uses to carry out its ministries. This is true for you, too. The understanding you have about how God thinks and acts influences the way you think and act; and the resources you will use as you go about your work in the church. The understanding you have about how God thinks and acts regarding conflict influences the way you think and act when conflict develops in your church. The place to begin in developing your conflict management skills, therefore, is to develop a sound theology regarding the place of conflict in the church.

WHAT IS THEOLOGY?

We often think theology is thinking about God in such a way as to understand His mysterious nature. As such, we assume only a few highly trained persons are theologians.

Theology, however, is more than thinking about God and His mysteries. Theology is the prayerful process of discerning how God may think and act in a given situation, in order that we may know how to think and act in such situations.

Theology is not merely concerned with far off, other worldly situations. It is concerned with here and now situations, and how we respond to them. Paul called upon every Christian to do the theological task when he said, "Do not be conformed to this world (do not mimick its way of thinking and acting) but be transformed by the renewing of your mind that you may prove what is the will of God (know how He thinks and acts, and wants you to think and act), Romans 12:2.

Each of us has a set of working assumptions about God which influences our thinking and doing. The theology you hold about conflict (your assumptions regarding how God thinks and acts in the midst of conflict) influences the way you will think and act when confronted by a conflict situation.

It is possible to have an incorrect theology regarding conflict (incorrect assumptions about God's thinking and acting regarding conflict) as well as to have a correct theology (correct assumptions about God's thinking and acting regarding conflict). Any study of conflict management in the church should, therefore, begin with a study of what scripture has to say about God and conflict in the church.

A THEOLOGY OF CONFLICT

I. THE TRAIL OF CONFLICT THROUGHOUT SCRIPTURE

1. The Beginning of Conflict: Genesis 3

Conflict came very early in human history. It started with a question, "Indeed, has God said, you shall not eat from any tree of the garden?" And then a statement, "You will not die. God knows if you eat it, you will be like Him."

Deep down inside, Eve experienced a tension she had not known before. Would she really be like God? Would she become wise? Would she die?

Eve's own desire to be greater than she was won over her value of obedience to God. She ate, and in that moment something inside of her died. This ended the first conflict episode in Scripture.

The first episode had hardly ended when the second began. Eve gave the fruit to Adam. He ate.

And God came calling, "Adam, where are you?"

"Over here, God, I'm hiding because I am naked and afraid."

"Who told you, you were naked? Have you eaten from the tree?"

"The woman made me do it."

"Woman, what have you done?"

"It's all the serpent's fault. He lied to me."

And the Lord God said to the Serpent, "because you have done this, you are cursed . . . ."

To the woman He said, "I will multiply your pain in childbirth . . . ."

And, to Adam, "cursed is the ground because of you and to dust you shall return . . . ."

With the argument finished, God lovingly covered their shame and for their future's good, put them out of the garden. Thus, the second episode of conflict ended.

We often read Genesis 3 and many other conflict situations in Scripture without ever realizing they actually are conflict situations. We miss the truth of these stories because we believe God and our great Bible heroes were above arguments and conflicts.

This is not the case. Take time now to read the story in Genesis 3. Pay attention to the words used, to the build up of tensions as the conversation continues to unfold, to the accusations and actions. This was no calm, friendly situation. No, indeed! These were personalities in conflict; wrongs had been committed, feelings had been hurt, tensions had developed in the relationships and in such a situation God, Himself, engaged in conflict.

2. The End of Conflict

Genesis 3 outlines the fall of humankind. From that time on Scripture describes humanity as living in a state of broken relationships with God and with one another. This is the curse of humanity. A curse which is finally corrected in Revelation 21 and 22 with the coming of a new kingdom in which "there shall no longer be any curse . . ." 22:3

Then, but not until then, shall all tears be wiped away, shall the child play at the snake's den, shall lion and lamb lay down together, and nations go to war no more.

But in the meantime, in all the time between Genesis 3 and Revelation 21 and 22, all human relationships, in the church as well as outside the church, will experience a tendency toward brokenness. There will be disagreements, misunderstandings, desires; some of which will result in conflict. Others will result not only in conflict, but also in sin.

3. In the "Meantime"

Conflict has become a normal part of human relationships. Persons conflict with each other, such as Cain with Abel, Genesis 4; and God conflicts with persons, such as in the days of Noah, Genesis 6:13, 14; and at the Tower of Babel, Genesis 11:5-9.

In the "meantime" all persons and organizations experience conflict. It is not limited to those who choose to live outside of God's will. In the New Testament, we are introduced to conflict inside the church. Here we see the very pillars of the church; Peter, Paul, Barnabas, the Lord Jesus, and many others disagreeing, experiencing conflict in their relationships.

The Book of Acts is the history of the birth and growth of the early church, and Acts 15 is the "conflict chapter" of the New Testament. The early church experienced tremendous conflicts in which Paul and Peter acted as some of the main conflictors. Listen to some of the phrases which describe the intensity of the conflict in Acts 15, "and Paul and Barnabas had great discension and debate with them . . ." v.2, "and after there had been much debate . . ." v.7." "There arose a sharp disagreement . . ." v.39. Remember they were not conflicting with outsiders but with fellow ministers of the Gospel.

Throughout the first conflict, vv. 1-31, Paul and Barnabas stood together, but no sooner was the first conflict settled than they fell into conflict between themselves so great they parted company, vv. 36-41.

Did these great apostles and missionaries fall into conflict because they were not spiritual enough, or because they were outside of God's will? Absolutely not! If the early church, with its great men and women of God experienced conflict, we can expect conflicts to arise in our churches and ministries also.

Some conflicts in the church result in sinful behavior, such as the inquisitions and the resulting assassinations; or a conflict in your own church which results in malicious backbiting and character assassination. On the other hand, some conflicts in the church result in a clearer understanding of the Will of God and in more effective ministries, as did the conflicts in Acts 15.

Jesus engaged in conflict. Sometimes He started conflict, such as the cleansing of the temple, Matthew 21:12-16. At other times He resolved conflict, such as in the situation of the woman found in adultery, John 8:3-11. And, at other times He avoided it, Luke 4:28-30.

If Jesus could not live in this world without conflict, we might as well accept it—we, too, will have conflict in our churches and ministries. Conflict is a normal part of the church in the "Meantime." Conflict, however, is not sinful of itself. Sinfulness in conflict results from the way we behave in the conflict, not from disagreement or tensions between us. Paul knew from personal experience there could be conflict without sin, and he encouraged us also to "be angry and do not sin," Ephesians 4:26.

II. UNDERSTANDING CONFLICT FROM A BIBLICAL POINT-OF-VIEW

As we consider what the writers of scripture have to say about conflict in the relationships of persons with God and with one another, it is important we recall they were writing as theologians; they were attempting to report conflict as God might think and feel about it. They were not alone in this effort. Indeed, we are told God worked with them in the writing; and these "holy" men of God spoke as they were moved by the Holy Spirit," II Peter 1:21. Their words regarding conflict were "given by inspiration of God," II Timothy 3:16. Following are some important things Scripture has to say about conflict. Please take the time to read and reflect on the words of each Scripture passage as you study your way through the following section.

A. Conflict as a Result of the Struggle to Understand God's Direction for Ministry; in such situations as segregation versus integration, and the necessary conditions for salvation and church membership.

1. Segregation vs. Integration. Should the Gospel be preached to the Gentiles, or is it for the Jews only? Acts 10:9-11:18.

What struggles the early church leaders had to go through to understand the "what, where, when and how" of God's leading for their ministry. Contrary to the conflicts which resulted from sin, these conflicts resulted from a desire to know and do the Will of God. In these conflicts God often becomes involved, 10:9-16.

Having settled the conflict between himself and God, Peter began to share the Gospel with the Gentiles, which promptly caused a conflict between himself and the other apostles, 11:1-3. And so it was in the midst of numerous conflicts that the church gained clarity about the direction of God's leading.

2. The Necessary Conditions Required for Salvation and Membership in the church. Acts 15:1-35.

Here is recorded a conflict between Paul, Barnabas and a group of other early evangelists. Again the issue concerned the Gentiles. Contrary to the Acts 11 issue, "should the Gospel be shared with the Gentiles?" the issue now was the conditions upon which the Gentile Christians should be accorded salvation and a place in the church.

The struggle to know how God might be thinking about the matter resulted in a conflict of such intensity it threatened to divide the entire church. The apostles finally called for a council in Jerusalem to settle the matter. Yet, in the very midst of the great dispute God was with them, blessing their ministry, 15:2, 3.

Was this conflict good or bad for the church? Did it come about because persons were pursuing sinful motives? Not at all, it came about because persons of differing opinions were trying to understand how God was thinking about the circumcision of Gentile Christians. It was a dangerous moment in the life of the early church, but the people demonstrated they could be in conflict without sin. And the Spirit of God never left them for a single moment.

B. Conflict as a Result of Differences Between Persons.

1. Paul and Barnabas, Acts 15:36-41. With the council at Jerusalem over, these two great missionaries set about to plan their next crusade only to find themselves in sharp disagreement over Mark—and they were both a bit stubborn about it. Barnabas was determined to take him along. Paul insisted they would not take him. The contention became so sharp they parted company.

The way the story is told to us, we gain little sense the two brothers were attempting to discover what God's intentions were about having Mark on their team. Each had his mind made up! Verses 36-40 tell us a lot about human nature and differences, even among the people of God. Verses 41 and 16:5 tell us a lot about God, His tolerance of our differences and His willingness to bless our ministries even when we are in conflict. I think this story about Paul and Barnabas falls under the category of the promise in II Corinthians 12:9, "My grace is sufficient for you, for My strength is made perfect in weakness."

2. The Corinthian Christians who were loyal to Paul and those loyal to Apollos, I Corinthians 1:10-12, 3:4-4:6. The congregation was divided. Some thought Paul was a more effective leader; others thought Apollos. The difference between them led to a great conflict. Had God abandoned them because of this difference? No, Paul insisted God was still there; living with them and within them, 3:16, 17. Paul made it clear God was not pleased with their petty differences, vv. 18-20, but he made it equally clear God had not withdrawn Himself from them because of it, "whether

Paul or Apollos or Cephas, or the world or life or death, or things present or things to come—all are yours. And you are Christ's in God," 3:22, 23.

C. Conflict as a Result of Sinful Motives.

1. David and Uriah, II Samuel 11. There came a brief moment in the life of David when he allowed his desire for sexual pleasure to take predominence over his desire to practice fidelity to God. One sinful motive lead to another until soon David fell into conflict with Uriah; finally plotting his death in order to preserve his own reputation, vv. 8-15.

2. Jesus and the Temple Money Changers, Matthew 21:12-16. Jesus initiated this conflict as a result of the sinful practices of those who had turned God's house of prayer into a place of personal profit.

Have you carefully read Matthew 21:12-14 to see all that happened in the temple that day? What a stark contrast between vv. 12 & 13 and v. 14. First is the conflict; then immediately "the blind and the lame came to Him in the temple and He healed them.

We often think a conflict in our church will weaken our ministry. This was not so in the life of Jesus, nor in the ministry of the early church. Acts 5:1-11 describes a fearful conflict between Annanias, Sapphira and Peter. Then, in the very next verse, we are told "and through the hands of the apostles many signs and wonders were done, and they were all with one accord."

THE SCRIPTURES PRESENT THREE BASIC TYPES OF CONFLICT AMONG GOD'S PEOPLE; CONFLICTS OVER PURPOSES AND GOALS, PROGRAMS AND METHODS, AND VALUES AND TRADITIONS.

A. Conflicts over Purposes and Goals.

1. Is the Gospel for the Jews only, or is it also for the Gentiles? Acts 10:9-11:18. This was a conflict to understand the purpose of God, and of the church, in terms of the Gentiles. Had God included the Gentiles in His plan of salvation? Did His plan include them or the Jews only?

2. Should Mark accompany the Missionary Team? Acts 15:36-41. This, too, was a conflict over purpose. It was Paul's contention that Mark's earlier behavior proved him a liability to the team, but Barnabas wanted to give him a second chance. Conflict!

B. Conflicts over Programs and Methods.

1. Must Gentile Christians be Circumcised? Acts 15:1-35. By what method could the Gentiles be saved—by faith only or was circumcision also necessary? Should the evangelistic program among the Gentiles include circumcision as well as baptism?

The issue here was not one of purpose, but of methods to achieve the purpose. The "purpose" question had been settled previously, Acts 10, 11. Now the issue was of methods to achieve that purpose.

2. What are the Legitimate Responsibilities of the Apostles and of the Disciples? Acts 6:1-7 gives us a brief account of another conflict involving program methods—how should the Christian widows be cared for by the church?

The Greek Christians were complaining their widows were being neglected. Apparently, all the disciples, Greek and Hebrew alike, thought it to be the apostles' responsibility to handle the daily distribution of goods to the widows. The apostles disagreed. Conflict!

As a result of this conflict, clarity was reached regarding the appropriate areas of responsibility for the apostles (pastors and missionaries) and for the disciples (believers). The first deacons were appointed, and there has grown all the ministries of all lay persons from then until now.

C. Conflicts of Values or Traditions.

1. David and Uriah II, Samuel 11. Sleeping with Bathsheba seemed to David to be a small matter. But when she became pregnant with Uriah away for several months, the whole affair escalated into a rather messy situation. People would be asking, "If not Uriah, then whom?"

David now valued his reputation above all else. He arranged for Uriah to come home—to sleep with Bathsheba. But Uriah valued his own oath of loyalty to his comrades in battle above all else. He would not engage in eating and pleasure while they were in battle. Conflict!

We see the extent to which David valued his own reputation when he finally plotted the death of this faithful soldier, vv. 14, 15.

2. Jesus and the Temple Money Changers, Matthew 21:12, 13. Here Jesus' value of purity in the house of God came into conflict with the long-time tradition of the temple leadership to profit from the need for worshippers to have doves for sacrifice and money for offerings. The worshippers were willing to pay for the convenience of buying the doves and making change right at the temple. This buying and selling, these tables for barter went against everything Jesus valued for the house of God. Conflict!

BIBLICAL UNDERSTANDINGS OF THE RESULTS OF CONFLICT.

A. Conflict in the Church can have Positive Results. The over-arching conclusion of Scripture is that well-managed conflict will often serve to strengthen the church's ministries.

The church generally responds to conflict in one of two ways: it either tries to ignore or avoid it; or attributes the conflict to a lack of spirituality among its members and then tries to preach and pray it away.

This is not the case in the biblical account of conflict in the early church. Its leaders neither ignored the conflicts nor attributed them to a lack of spiritual maturity among its members. The examples we have discussed here demonstrate they faced the conflicts head-on by bringing the disagreeing parties together, clarifying the issues and staying "together" until a manageable resolution had been hammered out.

In this manner, the early church leaders managed to turn potentially destructive conflicts into a greater clarity of God's will for the church and the discovery of new ministries to accomplish that will.

B. Conflict in the Church can Strengthen the Unity and Spirit its People, and when this is done the Spirit of God is given greater freedom to work through them.

Conflicts need not only highlight the points over which Christians disagree. It can often result in highlighting the points over which they strongly agree, thus bringing them together in a more concerted effort. Often a conflict over lesser values and purposes gets the people in touch once again with their higher values and purposes —and here they find agreement. In Acts 15, persons had strong disagreement over how the Gentiles were to be admitted into the church. They had forgotten the "higher value" which had been discovered in the Acts 10 and 11 conflict. But now, as they listened to the opposing parties, they considered again "the many miracles and wonders God had worked through them among the Gentiles," 15:12. Arguing ceased. People became calm and silent. A new, higher unity of purpose was born among them . . . .

C. Not all Conflict is Sinful. Conflict is a part of the human situation, and we must see it as a part of the Christian life. Scripture makes it clear the church is to honor the differences of its members, deal with them openly and seriously, and manage them so that the attitudes and behaviors of those who disagree do not result in sin.

It is no sin for persons in the church to be in conflict, but often when conflicts are ignored or poorly managed, they result in sinful behavior. When conflict spills over into character assassination ("the woman made me do it"), psychological or physical destruction (as David of Uriah), lying (as Annanias and Sapphira to Peter), it is sin. Whenever love is lost to hatred, gentleness to maliciousness, truthfulness to dishonesty, humility to selfishness; it is sin. But conflict free of such behavior is not sinful. It may be scary, embarrassing and dangerous, but yet without sin.

Develop an Understanding of Your Behavior in Conflict Situations

CONFLICT STYLES SURVEY

HOW TO PROCEED . . .Please read carefully.

In your organization you are active in one or more committees, groups or departments which are responsible for significant programs. The group(s) to which you belong must meet regularly to make decisions. In addition, all group members must assume responsibilities for carrying out the decisions.

Following are twelve situations you encounter; in some of the situations you are the group's leader, in others you are not the leader. For each situation you have five possible behavioral responses. Please study each situation and the possible responses carefully, then CIRCLE THE LETTER OF THE RESPONSE which you think would most closely describe your behavioral response to the situation.

As you complete the survey, please remember this is NOT a test. There are no right or wrong responses. The survey will be helpful to you only to the extent that you circle the responses which would be most characteristic of your conflict management behavior in that particular situation.

CIRCLE ONLY ONE CHOICE FOR EACH SITUATION!

SITUATION NO. 1:

YOU HEAD A TASK FORCE APPOINTED TO PLAN A LARGE CONFERENCE. ONE MEMBER HAS IDEAS VERY DIFFERENT FROM THOSE SUPPORTED BY THE REST OF THE GROUP. HE/SHE REFUSES TO GIVE EVEN A LITTLE BIT. TIME IS RUNNING OUT.

You Would: *(Circle one)*

A. Meet privately with the differing member to let him/her know you were not angry because of his /her position and encourage him/her, for the sake of future relationships, to become more flexible.

B. Ask the differing member to state why his/her ideas would result in a better conference. If he/she was unable to convince the group you would urge him/her to go along with the group's plan.

C. State that as leader of the group you do not want to make a unilateral decision, and call for a secret vote on the two plans.

D. Point out that much time had been spent in an attempt to resolve the differences and, since the majority of the group was in agreement, move ahead with the group's plan.

E. Ask the differing member to list points of disagreement with the group's plan, and to define why his/her ideas would result in a better conference. Then you would provide a process for the group to reevaluate its own plan in light of this information.

SITUATION NO. 2:

FROM YOUR POINT OF VIEW THE CHAIRPERSON OF YOUR COMMITTEE HAS INAPPROPRIATELY USED HIS/HER POSITION TO INFLUENCE A DECISION WITH WHICH YOU STRONGLY DISAGREE.

You Would: *(Circle one)*

A. Point out your perceptions to the group encouraging others to also reflect on the process by which the decision was reached. Press for policies to prohibit future inappropriate use of the chair's position.

B. Let the chairperson railroad the decision and simply let the group live with the results, since they allowed the chairperson such freedom.

C. Challenge the inappropriate behavior of the chairperson and move for a recall of the decision.

D. State your perceptions and ask the chairperson to defend the behavior. If after the defense you were still convinced chair's position had been used to influence the decision, you would move for a recall of the decision.

E. Rather than putting the chairperson "on the spot" in front of the group, you would bite your tongue and keep your feelings to yourself.

SITUATION NO. 3:

YOU ARE RESPONSIBLE FOR A PROGRAM WHICH IS STRONGLY SUPPORTED THROUGHOUT THE ORGANIZATION. YOU HAVE ANNOUNCED YOUR PLANS FOR THE COMING YEAR AND ARE BEING STRONGLY OPPOSED BY ANOTHER GROUP WHOSE OWN PROGRAM HAS PROVEN INEFFECTIVE.

You Would: *(Circle one)*

A. Prepare convincing information to support the need for your program ideas, communicate this to the entire organization, and proceed with your program as planned.

B. Feel your long-term relationship with the opposing group was more important than your program plans, and withdraw your plans.

C. Welcome the conflict as an opportunity to identify shared concerns and goals, and to promote better working relationships with the opposing group.

D. Attempt to find a solution that everyone could live with, by asking for an opinion by the top officials.

E. Meet with the group to explain your rationale for planning your program, inquire into the reasons for their opposition, and seek middle-ground agreements.

SITUATION NO. 4:

YOUR GROUP HAS MET OFTEN TO WORK ON PLANS FOR THE COMING YEAR. THERE IS MUCH DISAGREEMENT BETWEEN CERTAIN MEMBERS. YOU ARE AWARE CONFLICT IS BREWING.

You Would: *(Circle one)*

    A. Encourage the group to settle the differences so they might not interfere with the planning.

    B. Instruct the parties to get the differences out on the table in order that the entire group might search for mutually acceptable solutions.

    C. Tell them they don't all have to like each other, but they must work together to get the planning done.

    D. Reduce the tensions by allowing more time for informal conversation and schedule more breaks during the meetings to allow persons to get away from the work for a few minutes.

    E. Try to avoid open confrontation by sensing where persons are in relation to the issues and steering the discussion to consider middle ground alternatives.

SITUATION NO. 5:

YOU SERVE ON A STAFF OF THREE PERSONS. THE HEAD OF THE STAFF IS INSENSITIVE AND AUTOCRATIC. THE OTHER MEMBER IS VERY ANGRY. IT IS ONLY A MATTER OF TIME BEFORE HOSTILITIES WILL OCCUR BETWEEN THEM.

You Would: *(Circle one)*

    A. Tell them their behavior is interfering with staff effectiveness, insisting they lay their personal animosities aside and begin putting their energies into productive activity.

    B. Remain silent whenever they begin to argue, hoping they would work it out, or that the angry staff member would be able to fend for himself/herself.

    C. Encourage them to lay their hostilities aside since conflict of this intensity might leave deep personal scars.

    D. Try to avoid outright, hostile confrontation by emphasizing the need to reach agreement on roles and responsibilities that everyone could live with.

    E. Share your observations of their behavior, ask each of them to state their own opinions, and press for a redefinition of working relationships to reduce the hostilities.

SITUATION NO. 6:

AFTER MUCH CONFLICT, TWO GROUPS WITHIN THE CONGREGATION HAVE DEADLOCKED OVER PROPOSED USE OF SOME OF THE CHURCH BUILDING. YOU HAVE BEEN REQUESTED TO MEET WITH THEM TO ASSIST IN BREAKING THE DEADLOCK.

You Would: *(Circle one)*

    A. Consider both sides of the agreement before stating your solution to the problem.

    B. Encourage an open airing of their feelings and attempt to get the group to decide on a compromise plan everyone could live with.

    C. Encourage them to work through their differences, being careful not to cause unnecessary pain for themselves or the congregation.

    D. Remind them that as an "outsider" you actually could do very little to solve the problem, but you were willing to help in whatever way you could.

    E. Lead a process to allow airing of the differences, and to search for a mutually satisfactory alternative.

SITUATION NO. 7:

INFLUENTIAL MEMBERS HAVE BECOME DISSATISFIED WITH YOUR LEADERSHIP AND ARE INSISTING YOU RESIGN. SOME ARE THREATENING TO LEAVE IF YOU DO NOT. OTHERS ARE SUPPORTING YOU PRIVATELY, BUT ARE TAKING NO PUBLIC STAND.

You Would: *(Circle one)*

A. Inform the group you have no intention of resigning, and you want an open airing of the grievances in order that some middle ground may be reached.

B. Assume the public silence of some members indicates consent, and not wanting the group to lose any members, you would resign.

C. Determine the number demanding your resignation, and of your silent supporters. Having decided the majority was not calling for your resignation, you would announce your intention to stay.

D. Go to those opposing you to tell them you still care about them, and do whatever you could to restore good relationships.

E. Arrange a meeting with your opponents and supporters to discuss and search for ways to reduce the tensions and restore working relationships.

SITUATION NO. 8:

YOUR SECRETARY, A RESPECTED MEMBER OF YOUR CHURCH, HAS WORKED FOR YOU FOR ONE YEAR. THE QUALITY OF WORK IS VERY UNSATISFACTORY. YOU ARE GETTING A GROWING NUMBER OF COMPLAINTS.

You Would: *(Circle one)*

A. Encourage your secretary to identify anything in the office situation that may be adding to the problem, and agree upon steps to correct the situation.

B. Increase compliments for tasks satisfactorily done while gently pointing out the trouble spots.

C. Live with the situation a while longer, hoping your secretary would begin to catch on to the office work.

D. Point out the problems with work performance, and if after a reasonable time it was still unsatisfactory, you would fire him/her.

E. State your disapproval with the performance asking for your secretary's help to outline areas in which change was necessary, and steps to bring about improved performance.

SITUATION NO. 9:

YOUR GROUP IS CARRYING ON A VERY EFFECTIVE PROGRAM. SOME MEMBERS ARE ADVOCATING CERTAIN CHANGES BUT OTHERS ARE DECLARING THE CHANGES WILL WEAKEN THE PROGRAM. TENSIONS ARE RISING. YOU HAVE NO STRONG FEELINGS EITHER WAY.

You Would: *(Circle one)*

A. Encourage the group to settle their differences, being careful no one is hurt in the process.

B. Listen to all sides of the issues before deciding what steps to take to resolve the conflict.

C. Keep the opposing groups from outright confrontation by suggesting middle-of-the-road alternatives. If this failed, you would establish ground rules for avoiding deadlocks.

D. Bring the opposing sides together, define the issues as you see them, and suggest a process for resolving the conflict.

E. Allow the group to settle the matter on its own.

SITUATION NO. 10:

A CLOSE FRIEND WITH WHOM YOU WORK IS PUSHING FOR A DECISION WHICH YOU BELIEVE IS POTENTIALLY DAMAGING TO THE WORK OF THE ENTIRE ORGANIZATION.

You Would: *(Circle one)*

   A.   Demonstrate your unhappiness with his/her position by refusing to discuss the matter at all.

   B.   Refrain from stating how strongly you disagree, hoping he/she would change without being pushed to do so.

   C.   Openly express your disagreement, and together search to find a mutually acceptable position.

   D.   State your position on the matter attempting to negotiate a position both of you could live with.

   E.   State exactly why you think his/her position is unreasonable and dangerous, urging him/her to change the position.

SITUATION NO. 11:

YOU ARE A MEMBER OF A TASK FORCE APPOINTED TO PLAN A LARGE CONFERENCE. YOU HAVE IDEAS VERY DIFFERENT FROM THE REST OF THE GROUP, AND ARE CONVINCED YOUR PLAN WILL RESULT IN A BETTER CONFERENCE.

You Would: *(Circle one)*

   A.   Disagree but not argue since you were one against many. Neither would you feel obligated to publicly support their plan.

   B.   Encourage the group to review both plans, identify points of agreement and of disagreement, and press for alternatives to reflect the best features of both.

   C.   Use all the influence you had in the group to get your ideas incorporated into the final plan.

   D.   Outline your disagreements with the group's ideas and offer to join with them in building a compromise plan.

   E.   Go along with their ideas not wanting to block the group's work simply because you were not personally pleased with their plan.

SITUATION NO. 12:

YOU HEAD A COMMITTEE WHOSE EFFECTIVENESS DEPENDS UPON THE COOPERATION OF ANOTHER GROUP ENGAGED IN POWER AND AUTHORITY STRUGGLES WITH TOP LEADERS. THE CONFLICT IS EFFECTING THEIR PROGRAM, AND YOURS.

You Would: *(Circle one)*

   A.   Bring all the parties together to discuss the situation, seeing to it that the needs of your group were included in any agreement which was negotiated between the other group and top leaders.

   B.   Strengthen your own relationship with the other group by expressing understanding of their position, while at the same time being careful not to hurt relationships with top leaders.

   C.   Stay out of the conflict by structuring your program to be less dependent upon the support of the other group.

   D.   Bring the parties together to explain how the conflict was effecting your own program, and offer to mediate a mutually acceptable resolution of the conflict.

   E.   Meet with the group to point out that your own program was being adversely affected by their conflict with top leaders, and press for immediate solutions to the problem.

PLEASE TURN THE PAGE AND SCORE THE SURVEY ➡️

HOW TO SCORE THE SURVEY OF YOUR CONFLICT STYLES . . .

Order and Range of Style Preferences

1. On FIGURE 1.2.1, circle the same letter for each situation that you circled in your survey. (This designates the CONFLICT STYLE you chose for each situation.)
2. TOTAL the number of choices (circles) for each CONFLICT STYLE and enter sub-totals in the spaces provided for these SCORES.
3. Transfer these scores onto the SCORE column of FIGURE 1.2.2, in descending order of magnitude.
4. List the corresponding style names (FIGURE 1.2.1) in the STYLE column.

FIGURE 1.2.2 now provides you with two important insights into your conflict behavior:

1. A rank ordering of your CONFLICT STYLES PREFERENCES. The style receiving the highest score is the style you prefer most, etc.
2. The RANGE OF STYLES, or number of styles, you are able and/or willing to utilize.

These two pieces of information say something about your general philosophy and orientation toward conflict. For example, the style receiving the highest score will tend to be your preferred conflict behavior, the style with which you feel the least tension. The style receiving the second highest score will tend to be the style you will "fall back on" as the conflict tensions increase.

The number of times you chose each style suggests the strength of preference you give to each style.

SITUATIONS	YOUR RESPONSE CHOICES				
#1	(E)	A	C	D	B
#2	A	E	B	C	(D)
#3	(C)	B	D	A	E
#4	(B)	D	A	C	E
#5	(E)	C	B	A	D
#6	(E)	C	D	A	B
#7	(E)	D	B	C	A
#8	(A)	B	C	D	E
#9	(D)	A	E	B	C
#10	(C)	B	A	E	D
#11	B	E	A	C	(D)
#12	(D)	B	C	E	A
SCORES					
	Collaborating	Accommodating	Avoiding	Competing	Compromising
CONFLICT STYLES					

Figure 1.2.1

ORDER OF YOUR STYLE PREFERENCES		
CHOICE	STYLE	SCORE
1st		
2nd		
3rd		
4th		
5th		

Figure 1.2.2

INTERPRETING YOUR SCORES

Preferred and Back-Up Styles

The number of times you chose to use each style in response to the twelve situations indicates your preferred style (the one you choose most often), plus your back-up styles (those which you "fall back on" when your preferred style isn't effective in managing the conflict.

You will tend to enter every conflict with your preferred style. If, however, the conflict progresses and tensions increase, you will "fall back" on to your first back-up style.

If this style does not resolve the conflict and tensions within the situation, and within yourself, increase, even more you will "fall back" on your second back-up style, etc.

The number of times you selected a style in response to each of the twelve situations indicates the degree of preference, or the strength, you give to that style. A STYLE MUST HAVE BEEN SELECTED IN RESPONSE TO AT LEAST TWO OF THE SITUATIONS TO BE CONSIDERED A BACK-UP STYLE. All of the styles, then, with a score of two or more, make up your STYLE RANGE. If you selected only one or two styles two or more times, you perceive of yourself as having a limited range of conflict management behaviors.

If you selected three or four of the styles two or more times, you perceive of yourself as having a wide range of conflict management behaviors.

NOTE: As you now proceed to learn the meaning of the various conflict management styles, please keep these most important principles in mind:

1. Conflict management styles are learned, therefore, you can learn new ones, discard others, etc.

2. The collaborating style is the dominant style for conflict management. There are certain situations, however, when each of the other styles is appropriate.

3. Finally, WHATEVER score you achieved in the survey is not the most important consideration. It is more important that you go on from this point to learn to use collaborating as your dominant response to conflict and to learn in which types of situations it may be more appropriate for you to utilize one of the other styles.

There are yet some important discoveries awaiting you regarding how and when escalating tensions within a conflict situation, and within yourself, cause your conflict management behavior to change. This discussion must wait, however, until you have gained the learnings in Step 3 and Step 4. Then we will be able to pull it all together, pp. 37-39.

Develop an Understanding of Each Conflict Management Style

Conflict management is the process of influencing the activities and attitudes of an individual or group in the midst of disagreements, tensions, and behavioral actions which are threatening the relationship and/or the accomplishment of goals. We are all, therefore, conflict managers in many situations; as one attempting to reduce the tensions which have grown in relationship with another, as a group member attempting to influence the direction of a group in the midst of disagreement, etc.

The behaviors you employ in conflict have been learned over time and are consistent enough that others come to expect you to act in certain predictable ways whenever you experience conflict. Because conflict management styles are learned, they can be altered or replaced by new styles.

STOP!

For your own insight and learning it is imperative that you complete and score the survey, pp. 13-18, before reading any further in this book. Please complete the SURVEY before proceeding.

Many sets of titles have been coined to describe a variety of conflict management styles. Each style consists of a basic set of assumptions along with specific behaviors, gestures, expressions, and words that, when taken together, serve to comprise that particular style.

For example, if a person assumes church conflict is basically sinful and tends to do more harm than good, he/she will try to avoid conflict at all costs. And when conflict does develop, he/she will do whatever is possible to resolve the conflict as quickly as possible—even to the point of sacrificing his/her own goals or resigning the group.

Each of the conflict styles may be utilized with intentionality and a conscious decision to use it in a specific situation. Most persons, however, have given little thought to the styles they use. Rather, they adopt a conflict management style with little intentionality and are almost totally unconscious of the assumptions and behaviors which comprise that style.

The collaborating style is generally more appropriate and effective in managing conflicts than are the other styles. However, each of the other styles may be appropriate in certain situations.

The following pages describe each of the various conflict management styles and some of the assumptions and behaviors which comprise each style. These descriptions generalize. No one description "fits" anyone perfectly. These "portraits" are meant to identify and group certain assumptions and behaviors so that you may learn to be more intentional about your own behavior in conflict situations—choosing to keep certain styles of behavior, learning some new ones, discarding others.

DESCRIPTIONS OF CONFLICT MANAGEMENT STYLES

As you study the following material keep in mind that the *collaborating style is generally more appropriate than the others. However, in certain situations each of the other styles may be appropriate.*

The "titles" used to identify each style are illustrative only and are not definitive.[1] Actually, it would do no harm to the survey or the entire study if no such terms were used at all and you simply relied upon the definitions for an understanding of the styles.

[1] The terms used here are adopted from "Conflict and Conflict Management," Kenneth Thomas, Vol. II. *The Handbook of Industrial and Organizational Psychology*, Marvin Dunnette, ed., Rand McNally, 1975.

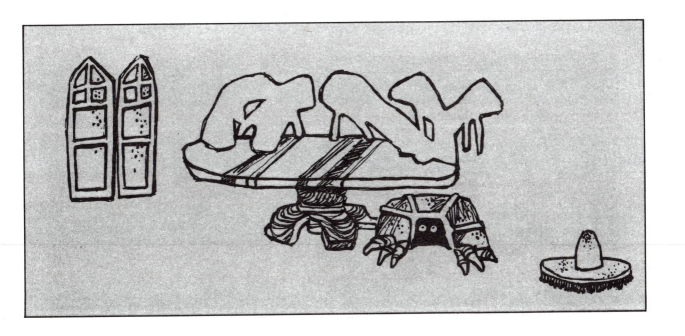

AVOIDING

The intent of this style is to stay out of the conflict, to avoid being identified with either side. The use of this style creates a situation in which other persons must assume responsibility for resolving the conflict issues. In order to do this, the person will become more or less passive in the face of the conflict and, in some cases, may withdraw from the conflict scene altogether.

The use of this style requires the person to be unassertive; neither pursuing his/her own interests in the situation, nor supporting others to achieve their interests. The person will not cooperate in defining the conflict, seeking a solution, or in carrying it out.

Other terms which have been used to define this type of conflict behavior are: passive, abdicating, lose-leave, the turtle.

The message communicated by this behavior is, "I don't care enough about the issue to invest time and energy into solving it," or "even though I care, it is not appropriate for me to become involved. It is someone else's problem."

This style may be adopted because the individual sees the issue as trivial, that there are more important issues to be dealt with, or because the issue is seen as hopeless and to become involved will only lead to endless struggles which he/she cannot win.

As a conflict style, avoiding can be exhibited in varying degrees, from a situation in which the individual is physically present but restrains from becoming involved in the conflict, to one in which he/she withdraws completely from the conflict setting. In the first instance, the person will participate in group affairs but will become silent and withdrawn whenever the conflict issue is approached. In the latter situation, the person will physically leave the group.

Possible effects of long term, consistent use of this style are a sense on the part of the other party of being always right, and of the prerogative to have his/her way in every situation. For the party employing the avoiding style, there is a cumulated sense of frustration and weakness, compliance without commitment, and, finally, deep-seated hostility.

ACCOMMODATING

The intent of this style is to preserve the relationship at all cost. To insure this, the individual will deny or avoid conflict whenever possible. When it is no longer possible, he/she will attempt to quickly resolve the conflict by taking whatever steps are necessary in order to run least risk of hurting others or damaging relationships.

The person actively seeks to "sweep the conflict under the carpet" by appealing to all parties to "forgive and forget." When this doesn't work, he/she will seek to appease others by conceding his/her own interests, or those of the organization, by confessing full "blame" and begging forgiveness, by seeking to accommodate the other person's desires.

The use of this style requires the person to be assertive in seeking solutions which are acceptable to others while being unassertive regarding one's own interests.

Other terms which have been used to define this type of conflict behavior are person oriented, yield-lose, the teddy bear.

The message communicated by this behavior is, "Our getting along with each other is more important than the issue over which we are in conflict."

This style may be adopted because the person genuinely cares more for the relationship than about his/her stakes in the issue—and feels good about it; or because he/she sees others as so fragile they cannot work through genuine differences without "breaking," therefore to openly confront the differences will almost certainly damage relationships.

The style may also be adopted because the person sincerely sees him/herself to be wrong, or sees the issue to be of greater importance to the other person, therefore to concede will do no damage to his/her own interests in the situation.

Possible effects of consistent, long-term use of this style are very different for the two parties. The party who is consistently accommodated will feel vindicated for his/her part in the conflict, will become more aggressive in presenting demands and will come to see the other person as weak and unstable. The person consistently employing this style, however, will come to present a false front of cooperation, cheerfulness, and love for the other person; will think less of him/herself; and will come to feel a terrible responsibility to maintain the relationship at whatever personal cost.

COLLABORATING

The intent of this style is to get all the parties fully involved in defining the conflict and in carrying out mutually agreeable steps for managing the conflict. In order to do this, the person puts equal, high emphasis on achieving the goals of all the members, safeguarding the interests of the organization, and on maintaining the well-being of the relationship. This style has a commitment to the idea that all goals must be served if the relationship is to endure.

In order to accomplish this, the person is assertive, yet flexible, in keeping the differing parties in communication, and is committed to the premise that conflict can be managed in such a way as to strengthen the organization and relationships. Conflict is not to be ignored or avoided; rather, it is to be turned into a problem-solving situation in which all can participate in finding solutions.

Other terms which have been used to define this type of conflict behavior similar to that described here are: activating, total involvement, synergistic, win-win, the owl.

The message communicated by this behavior is, "Everyone's goals are important, and if we work together we will find mutually acceptable approaches to the conflict issue."

This style is adopted when all parties are esteemed as persons of value, when both sets of concerns are too important to be ignored, and/or the cooperation and commitment of others will be important to implement any satisfactory solution.

This style is based upon the assumption that persons are capable of confronting differences without being personally hurt or hurting the relationship. The style also assumes that a cooperative working through of differences will arrive at more creative solutions than could be achieved by any single person.

Possible effects of consistent, long-term use of this style are increased trust, stronger relationships, mutually enthusiastic implementation of the agreed-upon solution, and increased goal achievement.

COMPROMISING

The intent of this style is to provide each side with a little bit of winning in order to persuade each to accept a little bit of losing. It is based on the assumption that while it is impossible for everyone to be fully satisfied, it is nonetheless desirable for the "common good" that the parties continue in relationship.

This style requires the person to be assertive but not inflexible in order to arrive at a solution which spreads the winning and the losing around as evenly as possible. Persuasion and, if necessary, manipulation are used in order to partially satisfy the needs of both sides by allowing everyone to be heard, and to avoid a situation where either side can block progress toward "splitting the difference."

Other terms which have been used to define this type of conflict behavior are: negotiation, bargaining, conciliation, win a little-lose a little, the fox.

The message communicated by this style is, "We must all submit our personal desires to serve the 'common good' of both parties and the larger community."

This style may be adopted when the goals of both sides are moderately important but not worth aggression, when a "standoff" may cause greater harm to all persons concerned, time pressures do not allow a search for more creative, mutually satisfying solutions, or when the two opponents are of mutual strength and are firmly committed to differing goals.

Possible effects of consistent, long-term use of this style are "cool," strained relationships, half-hearted commitment to the agreed-upon solution, limited goal attainment, and recurring conflicts under the guise of new issues.

A Special Word About Compromise—The compromising style warrants special attention in light of the different views religious organizations have toward "compromise" as compared to those of secular organizations. Secular organizations often hold an extreme, almost fanatical bias in favor of compromise, while religious organizations often hold an extreme, almost fanatical bias against it. Both positions are overdone and unnecessary.

In secular institutions, especially governmental and legal, a compromise mentality has become so ingrained that any other approach to a conflict issue is hardly considered. Eloquent oratory regarding the essential "goodness' of compromise is often used to support negotiations and bargains. These persons lump everything from the democratic process to "playing by the rules of the game" under compromise procedures.

Among Christians, the very word "compromise" often evokes connotations of sinful duplicity, lowering of standards, "selling out" to evil. Eloquent oratory regarding the essential evil of compromises is often used to support a hard-line position.

As Christians, we must never compromise our faith with evil. It is often appropriate, however, to compromise with each other when no sin or evil intent is involved.

COMPETING

The intent of this style is to win. The person operates out of a basic philosophy that there are only two possible outcomes in conflict, winning and losing—and winning is better than losing.

The person generally does not desire to hurt others, nor to damage the relationship. He/she simply places prime importance on personal goals or upon his/her interpretation of what is best for the organization and, if necessary, will sacrifice the relationship in order to accomplish this.

This style requires the individual to be aggressive, domineering, and generally uncooperative in the pursuit of any solution except his/her own. Often the person's own sense of self esteem is involved, therefore he/she must seek to win at any cost.

Other terms which have been used to define this type of conflict behavior are: task oriented, domineering, controlling, win-lose, the shark.

The message communicated by this style is, "I know what's best for all parties concerned and for the organization."

This style assumes persuasion, power, and coercion are legitimate methods in conflict. It may be adopted when quick, vital decisions must be made; important, unpopular policies must be implemented; or when the person believes beyond all doubt that his/hers is the best solution.

The style does not necessarily require the person be ruthless. The behavior may range from that of paternalistic, benevolent dictator; to that of an iron-fisted autocrat.

Possible effects of consistent, long-term use of this style are acquiescence, increasing covert hostility, half-hearted implementation of the solution, and decreased goal achievement.

27

Discover the Basic Concerns Which Determine Your Conflict Management Styles

How is it that each of us comes to prefer one particular conflict style above the others? What causes one person to prefer (be most comfortable with) competing behavior while another prefers accommodating behavior?

Most conflict studies support the idea that we each learn to prefer a particular style as we observe conflicts and their results in our own lives, and in the lives of others. These studies also agree there are two fundamental concerns which affect each person's behavior in a conflict situation.

THE TWO FUNDAMENTAL CONFLICT CONCERNS[1]

In one way or another, all conflict studies deal with two fundamental concerns of every person engaged in conflict:

1. Concern for the relationships of the persons engaged in, or affected by, the conflict. What will this conflict do to the people? What will it do to our relationships?

2. Concern for one's own personal goals/interests within the area of conflict. What will this conflict do to my goals and interests, both for myself and for the organization?

Figure 1.4.1 illustrates these two concerns.

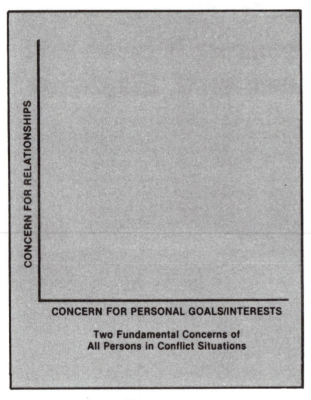

Figure 1.4.1

These are the two essential concerns which each person brings, consciously or subconsciously, to every conflict situation. Each individual attaches a certain degree of importance to each concern. One person, for example, has learned that in conflict winning is the most important thing, while another person has come to believe that maintaining friendly relationships is most important. The first person will engage in conflict in such a way as to ensure his/her own personal goals/interests are accomplished even at the expense of the relationship, if necessary. This is the essential foundation of the competing style. The orientation is to take care of one's personal interests—to take care of oneself even at the expense of other persons.

The second person, however, will engage in the conflict in such a way as to ensure persons are not "hurt" by the conflict and that relationships are not damaged—even at the expense of his/her own personal goals/interests, if necessary. This is the essential foundation of the accommodating style. The orientation is to take care of the other people even at the expense of taking care of oneself.

A third person may have little or no commitment to maintaining the relationship or to any personal goals in the situation. This is the essential foundation of the avoiding style.

A fourth may hold high commitment to maintaining both the relationship and to achieving the personal goals/interests of all parties in the conflict. This is the essential foundation of the collaborating style.

There is yet a fifth possibility, that of a person who is willing to support the personal goals/interests of all the parties involved to whatever extent necessary to keep the relationship together, however imperfect it may be. This is the essential foundation of the compromising style.

These are five possible combinations of the two fundamental conflict concerns. The figure (1.4.1) illustrating the two fundamental concerns can now be expanded to depict the five combinations. See Figure 1.4.2.

[1] This model for illustrating combinations of conflict management concerns was developed by Robert Blake and J.S. Mouton and is known as the "Managerial Grid." See R.R. Blake and J.S. Mouton, "The New Managerial Grid," Houston Gulf Publishing Company, 1978.

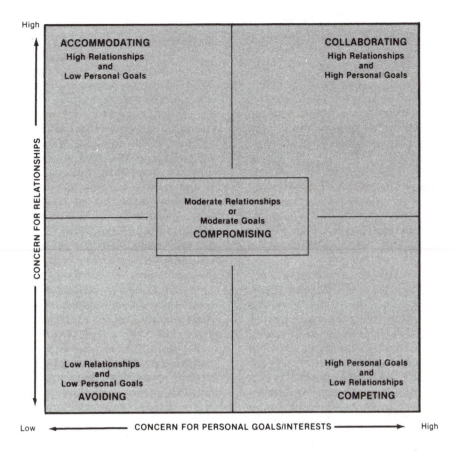

Figure 1.4.2

THE APPROPRIATENESS AND EFFECTIVENESS OF EACH CONFLICT MANAGEMENT STYLE

Most persons never consciously consider the appropriateness or effectiveness of their conflict styles. Rather they tend to prefer one over the other because they have learned it is the style which best reduces the tension they feel while in the conflict situation.

All conflict is threat producing. What is being threatened are the personal relationships which are important to the individual, and the achievement of his/her personal goals/interests in the situation. This tension is aggrevated by a thorny dilemma—if the person puts too much emphasis on maintaining warm, friendly relationships he/she runs the risk of sacrificing his/her own goals and interests. On the other hand, if one presses too hard for his/her own goals and interests at the expense of other's, he/she is almost certain to damage the relationship.

In the midst of these concerns and tensions

each of us, by observing others, by listening to what others have to say about conflict, and by personal trial-and-error, come to accept one style as our preferred method for reducing the tension we experience in conflict. This is generally done at a subconscious level. Few persons have ever seriously thought about such things as a "preferred style," or "my two fundamental concerns in conflict."

The effectiveness of a conflict style, however, should not be measured only by the degree to which it reduces tension inside one's self. It should also be measured by the short- and long-term effects it will have upon the people and the organization. Any style will, of course, produce short-term effects when used only once. But using any style on an occasional basis will generally not produce any long-term effects.

In specific short-range situations, no conflict style is better or worse than the others, per se. There is no "ideal" style which is most appropriate or effective in all short-range isolated situations.

However, any style used consistently over a period of time will produce long-term effects—good or ill.

Over the long-haul, the collaborating style is to be preferred above the others. It is the style which commits persons to do everything necessary to see to it that the personal relationships remain strong, that lines of communication remain open, that all persons' goals and interests are honored. In this manner, conflict serves to strengthen member-ties, unleash the creativity of all the people, and commit all the members to a whole-hearted support of the organization's best interests.

Having said all that about the collaborating style, let me say something that may sound quite to the contrary.

Sometimes a person may choose a style other than collaborating not only for its short-term effects but also because in that particular situation it may produce more positive long-term results. For example, when the party with whom you are in conflict simply does not possess the psychic energy and self-esteem necessary to contribute creatively to the problem solving process, it may be appropriate to adopt the accommodating style; to give up your own short-range goals and interests in order to demonstrate respect and acceptance of the person's ideas, without causing any additional tension.

Also, few persons will have the time or energy to work the collaborating style in every conflict situation. For example, when you sincerely believe your ideas are best for the future of the organization, but some persons are strongly resisting, and time is running out, competing may be the most appropriate style.

REFLECTIONS ON YOUR SURVEY RESULTS:
Preferred and Back Up Styles

The survey helped you identify the conflict management style you prefer to use, and the style(s) you generally "fall back" on as a conflict "heats up" and the tensions increase. **Indeed, your back up styles may be a far more important consideration than your preferred style.** The fact you have a preferred style does not mean you cannot or will not use the other styles. Indeed, it is a safe assumption that everyone uses all of the styles at various times. A major intent of this study is not simply to make you aware of your preferred and back up style, but to:

1. Make you aware that several other styles also exist.

2. Convince you that one should intentionally decide upon the most appropriate style to use in each situation, taking into account short- and long-term effects.

3. Encourage you to expand your style range; the number of styles you can effectively use.

Your preferred style tells you something important regarding your views of, and behavior in conflict. **Your first (and second) back up style, however, may tell you even more. It is your back up style(s) that tells you how you actively behave when the conflict is highly threatening and tensions are mounting.** What do you do under such circumstances? Do you tend to withdraw, give up your interests in order to save the relationship, or do you "come on strong?" Your choice of back up styles tells you how you tend to react under increasing conflict pressure; whether you become more flexible, more soft, more analytical, more rigid.

As you continue your way through this study, ponder your survey results, and the results of the exercises you are asked to complete. Study the material in this book and on the tape over and over again until it "gets inside of you." As you study the material and ponder the implication of your own views and behaviors in conflict, remember CONFLICT MANAGEMENT STYLES ARE LEARNED. Therefore, you can develop styles which you are not now using, "trade in" your presently preferred style for a new one, and change the order of your back up styles.

For you to become more effective in conflict management requires that you become aware of the styles that are available and of their consequences—and possibly to undertake a conscious program for change in the way you behave in conflict situations.

YOU ARE NOT LOCKED INTO YOUR PRESENT VIEWS, RESPONSES AND RESULTS IN CONFLICT.

We will return to a discussion of your conflict management styles at the conclusion of your study of the next step, p. 37.

Understanding How Conflict Develops, and How to Manage It

In this section you will:

STEP 1: Learn the Stages of Conflict
as it Becomes More Intense

STEP 2: Learn the Basic Skills of Conflict Management

STEP 3: Apply Your Learnings to Conflict Situations

LEARNING EXERCISE NO. 1:
The Long Range Effects of Consistently Utilizing
One Conflict Management Style

LEARNING EXERCISE NO. 2:
Reflecting on Conflict Situations to Identify
Conflict Management Styles Utilized by Yourself

SECTION II
MANAGING CONFLICT

Step 1

Learn the Stages of Conflict as it Becomes More Intense

Conflict is two or more objects aggressively trying to occupy the same space at the same time:[1] two cars trying to get into the same parking space; two persons each trying to have his "own way" regarding an important decision; or, two lions claiming the same territory.

Conflict arises when the actions of one party threatens the values, goals, or behaviors of another party. Conflict always involves (1) Action; (2) Threat; and (3) Reaction.

ACTION: The behavior of one party;

THREAT: Threatens to take, damage or destroy a "territory" which is claimed by another party; thus:

REACTION: Causing the threatened party to react in ways intended to protect his claim on the territory.

---

[1] G. Douglass Lewis, *Resolving Church Conflicts: A Case Approach for Local Congregations*, New York: Harper & Row, 1981.

35

CHANGE: THE SEEDBED OF CONFLICT

No relationship can exist very long without disruptions to persons' expectations of one another. These disruptions are the seed-bed for conflict, and come about because of the constant changes going on, many of which are beyond our control; persons grow older, the congregation grows larger (or smaller), members move away or die, new persons assume positions of leadership, communities change.

Uncontrollable change is going on within every church family, every church board, and within the entire congregation. The agreements and programs agreed to last year now seem to some to be outmoded or confining, others feel they are more important than ever. It is these changes in persons' attitudes and behavior which cause conflict to begin in the first place. Conflict is born in the changes within one person's attitudes or actions which prevents, blocks, interferes with, injures, or in some way makes the achievement of another person's goals less likely.

THE CONFLICT CYCLE

Once begun, conflict follows a five stage progression. The length of time for any stage may be very short (a few minutes) to very long (several months), but no stage is missed.

The conflict may be handled at any stage. If it is not, it will progress to the next stage. Following is an illustration of how conflict begins and progresses through the various stages:

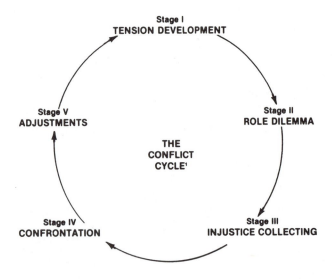

Stage I
TENSION DEVELOPMENT

Stage II
ROLE DILEMMA

THE
CONFLICT
CYCLE¹

Stage III
INJUSTICE COLLECTING

Stage IV
CONFRONTATION

Stage V
ADJUSTMENTS

THE STAGES OF CONFLICT

TENSION DEVELOPMENT

All conflict begins as a mere tension in the relationship. The tension signals that someone is experiencing a sense of loss of freedom within the relationship—and this sensed loss of freedom sets the stage for a conflict situation.

Resolution of the conflict is handled most effectively at this stage since little or no harm has occurred to the participants. Unfortunately, it is not often handled at this stage because participants are embarrassed to mention the presence of the tensions since the issues seem so insignificant.

If the tensions are not openly admitted and managed, after a while confusion will set in because persons feel they can no longer depend on one another to do what is expected of them. Further, their own appropriate role and behavior is unclear to them in the new situation. Harmony and productivity give way to role dilemma which begins to consume persons' time and energies.

ROLE DILEMMA

Confusions that develop as a result of the tension arouses such questions as, "What am I doing to cause this tension? What is he/she doing? What's happening here? Who's in charge?"

Now, as never before, the persons should be talking to one another; defining the points of tension, identifying the changes which have caused the tension, and using this as new information upon which to renegotiate new commitments before the problem gets any worse.

Paradoxically, however, few persons or groups will openly discuss the disruptive influences at the tension development or the role dilemma stages. At the tension development stage the issues seem so insignificant they are embarrassed to lay it out on the table for examination, while at the role dilemma stage, the issues already appear so threatening they choose to avoid it. By now the tensions have increased to the point that communications are beginning to break down and persons are actively blaming one another. This opens the door to injustice collecting.

¹ The illustration of the Conflict Cycle suggested by Jerry Robinson, Jr. and Roy A. Clifford, *Managing Conflict in Community Groups*, University of Illinois, 1974.

INJUSTICE COLLECTING

This is the first dangerous stage. Now the people are convinced matters can only get worse, so they begin pulling apart and preparing for the "battle" which they are certain will come sooner or later. They begin collecting injustices and hurts which will be used as "artillery" later.

Injustice collecting generates negative energy which must be spent before persons will ever again be able to focus on the issue rather than on the "enemy."

This is the "blaming" stage when persons begin justifying their own position and pointing out it is all the other party's fault.

Here persons are looking for reasons to pull apart, to put distance between themselves and those on the other side of the issue. This distancing happens because at this stage persons begin taking their attention off the conflict issue and begin focusing on the other party.

Now the other is the problem, and reason gives way to anger.

CONFRONTATION

Confrontation may range from "clearing the air" to outright violence. In unmanaged conflict persons confront each other. In well managed conflict they confront the issues which caused the tension in the first place.

This is the fight or "contact" stage. The battle lines are set and the conflict erupts. The "contact" stage is inevitable only after injustice collecting has gone on for some time.

Confrontation under unmanaged or poorly managed conditions is usually even more fearful than imagined—and it does not solve the problems. Persons are now confronted with a set of less-than-desirable alternatives; they can sever the relationship, attempt to return to the way things used to be, or they can negotiate a new set of expectations and commitments. However, such negotiation is always done under pressure because the persons feel there is no other viable alternative.

ADJUSTMENTS

Adjustments are the changes people make to end the confrontation.

Adjustments made in poorly managed confrontations take such forms as avoidance, divorce, domination, cold war.

Adjustments made in well managed confrontations will take the form of renegotiated expectations and freely made commitments to honor the expectations.

THE EFFECTS OF PROGRESSIVE CONFLICT UPON YOUR CONFLICT MANAGEMENT STYLE

NOTE: The materials following may be your most important learnings in the entire course. Please study it carefully!

The key consideration in understanding the conflict cycle is that conflict is dynamic; if it is not effectively managed at any particular stage it will progress to the next. The single most important factor causing this progression is increasing tension in the organizational situation and/or in the interpersonal relationships.

This same tension which causes the conflict to progress through the stages also causes one to abandon his/her preferred conflict management style in favor of using his/her back up style(s).

This is always the situation for a person who has never thought about the fact that he/she does have a preferred and back up style(s), and who simply responds to the increasing tension by more-or-less subconsciously altering behavior in an attempt to reduce the tension.

This need not be the case for you. You are now consciously aware of your preferred conflict style, and of the patterns of change in behavior you have tended to follow in conflicts which become progressively more tension producing. Now that you know this about yourself you need no longer follow those patterns. You may consciously choose to not use your preferred style, or you may choose to stick with a style throughout an entire conflict situation regardless how much tension you may be feeling.

You can consciously decide which style will likely have the best short- and/or long-range effects, and use it. To do so will not reduce the tension you feel, but it will allow you to achieve more effective conflict resolutions. When you alter your behavior simply because of the tension you are feeling, the conflict is controlling you. When you approach the conflict with a conscious decision regarding the management style you are going to use, you are in control of yourself, and are in better position to manage the entire situation toward positive results.

COMBINING YOUR CONFLICT STYLE SCORES WITH THE CONFLICT STAGES

It is now possible to combine your conflict survey scores, p. 18, with the conflict stages to give you some indication of how much tension you may experience before "falling back" on a different style of conflict management behavior. To do this, please transfer the information from Figure 1.2.2, p. 18, to Figure 2.1.1, below.

Now refer to Figure 2.1.2, p. 39, to provide the additional information needed to complete the right hand portion of the chart below.

	ORDER OF YOUR STYLE PREFERENCES			STYLES YOU GENERALLY USE AT EACH STAGE			
Choice	Style	Score		TD	RD	IC	C
1st		10					
2nd		✓					
3rd							
4th							
5th							

Figure 2.1.1

Studying the information of your own style preferences and the strength you give to each style (score), Figure 2.1.1, above, tells you a great deal about the extent to which you may be using your preferred style. For example, according to Figure 2.1.2, if you chose your preferred style less than eight times (out of a possible twelve), you probably never use it in conflicts that are very serious (injustice collecting or confrontation). Even though you would prefer to act this way in serious conflict, the degree of tension you feel has already driven you to your first back up style, if you chose it at least three times. If you did not, and if you have a second back up style, you are probably already using it by the time the conflict reaches injustice collecting.

But it need not be this way. And you may, if you wish, begin to make necessary changes to move you toward more effective conflict management behavior.

Effective conflict management calls for one to be heavily committed to collaboration but not so much as to be unable to compromise when necessary. One must also be able to take firm competitive stands when nothing else will get the job done, and to be able to accommodate, or even to avoid the conflict issue altogether when such a style will produce the best long-range results.

IF YOUR STYLE SCORES ARE:	YOU WILL TEND TO USE THAT STYLE AT: (X = STAGES)			
	Tension Development	Role Dilemma	Injustice Collecting	Confrontation
Preferred Style Scores				
10-12	X ————————————————————————→			X
7-9	X ——————————————————→		X	
4-6	X ——————→	X		
First Back-up Scores				
5-6		X ————————————————————→		X
3-4			X ——————→	X
2				X
Second Back-up Scores				
2-3				X

NOTE: In determining which style you would tend to use, the second back-up scores take precedence over all other scores, and the first back-up scores take precedence over the preferred style scores.

Figure 2.1.2

**LEARNING EXERCISE NO. 1: The Long-Range Effects of Consistently Utilizing
One Conflict Management Style.**

Part I:

While I was preparing this study, Dave Jones attended one of our conflict training sessions in which the group was asked to write about the most serious conflicts they had experienced in ministry.

Following are abbreviated accounts of the most serious conflicts Dave has faced in his ministry. Please read them carefully.

Conflict Situation No. 1

Date: 1972-1974; *Conflict Setting:* My first pastorate.

Conflict Situation: The conflict developed over the loyalty of the congregation to the preceding pastor, and his lack of ministerial ethics. A group within the church remained in close contact with him after I came. He returned to visit the people four or five times. I was a novice pastor and all of this threatened me a great deal.

I internalized my anger, becoming subdued and passive. Then, after two years, I began to suffer physically and psychologically and resigned the church. I carried the feelings and scars of this conflict to my next church.

Conflict Situation No. 2

Date: 1976; *Conflict Setting:* My second pastorate.

Conflict Situation: The conflict developed over my responsibility of myself, as pastor, to "unfaithful" members.

A child died just at the time I was to leave for the General Assembly session of our denomination. The father's name was on our church roll; however, he never attended any services or participated in church functions. The mother attended another church.

Upon learning of the death I attempted to contact the family. I could not locate them, however, and decided to leave for General Assembly.

Upon my return I found the church in an up-roar. The family was hostile because "I left just when the family needed me." The board had met to consider firing me.

Feeling my ministry had been discredited, I became dissolutioned and left the pastoral ministry for a teaching position at a Bible college within a different denomination. Also, some of my old unresolved theological problems surfaced again, resulting in my changing denominations.

Conflict Situation No. 3

Date: 1982

Conflict Situation: The college experienced a change of presidents. Several students and one vocal, irate parent registered complaints with the new president about my "doctrinal teaching" from 1979-1981.

I gave written statements of my belief to the new president, the local denominational executive, and the college academic dean. After communication with the executive committee of the denomination, the denominational executive said the problem would have to be solved in the school. The college president, however, said I would have to be examined by the denomination's executive committee.

This left me feeling the church was incapable of giving me any support locally or nationally. I felt insecure and began seeking ordination in another denomination. This was granted and I left the school to begin pastoring in the new denomination.

Part II:

Review the three conflict situations and write your responses to the following questions.

1. What words did Dave use to describe the tensions he felt within himself while in the conflicts?

2. Specifically, what did he do in response to the tensions:
   —in Situation No. 1?

   —in Situation No. 2?

   —in Situation No. 3?

3. What prevailing patterns do you see in Dave's feelings and actions when in conflict?

4. Study the definitions of conflict styles, pages 23-27, to determine what style(s) Dave utilized in these conflicts.

5. Describe the short-range effects to Dave as a result of his preferred conflict style.

6. Describe the long-range effects to Dave as a result of his preferred conflict style.

LEARNING EXERCISE NO. 2: Reflecting on Conflict Situations to Identify Conflict Management Styles Utilized by Yourself.

Part I:

INSTRUCTIONS: On separate sheets of paper, reconstruct two or three most serious conflict situations *in which you were involved as an active participant* in the conflict.

For each situation write your responses to the following items:

1. Describe the conflict situation: What was the conflict issue? Who were the persons/groups involved? What position did each take? What were the outcomes of the conflict?

2. Reflect upon your own part in the conflict (be specific in providing the following information): What word or words would best describe your feelings during the conflict? What were your major concerns or fears? In your opinion (then, not now) what was the best solution? Above all else, what did you want to see happen, no matter what approach was finally taken to resolve the conflict?

3. Specifically, jot down what you did and said to resolve the conflict.

4. Now, remembering what you wrote in Nos. 2 and 3 above, study the definitions of conflict styles, pages 23-27, to determine: the style(s) you utilized in this conflict. What indicators in your own concerns, feelings, actions, words are you using to identify your style?

5. Specifically, what were the results of your using this style (or styles) for yourself? for the other parties?

6. If you had it to do over would you utilize a different conflict management style? Which one would you use? Why do you think this style might be preferable over the one you used?

Part II:

INSTRUCTIONS: On separate sheets of paper, reconstruct two or three serious conflict situations in which *you were not directly involved* as an active participant, *but you did become involved in seeking to help resolve it*.

For each situation write your responses to the following items:

1. Describe the conflict situation: What was the conflict issue? Who were the persons/groups involved? What position did each take? What were the outcomes of the conflict?

2. Reflect upon your own part in the conflict (be specific in providing the following information): What word or words would best describe your feelings during the conflict? What were your major concerns or fears?

3. Specifically, jot down what you did and said to help the conflicting parties resolve the conflict.

4. Now, remembering what you wrote in Nos. 2 and 3 above, study the definitions of the conflict styles, pages 23-27, to determine: What style(s) you utilized in this conflict? What indicators in your own concerns, feelings, actions, words are you using to identify your style?

5. Specifically, what were the results of your using this style (or styles) for the persons who were directly involved in the conflict?

6. If you had it to do over would you utilize a different conflict management style? Which one would you use? Why do you think this style might be preferable over the one you used?

Part III:

INSTRUCTIONS: On the chart below identify the style you used in each conflict situation.

Those in which you were directly involved as a conflict participant.

For each conflict situation, place an "X" in the box that will identify the conflict management style you used, see No. 4, Parts I & II.

Conflict Situation No. 1

Conflict Situation No. 2

Conflict Situation No. 3

Those in which you were involved in helping to seek a solution.

Conflict Situation No. 1

Conflict Situation No. 2

Conflict Situation No. 3

Totals:

	Avoiding	Accommodating	Collaborating	Competing	Compromising

1. Which style did you use most frequently when you were directly involved in the conflict?

   _____

2. Which style did you use most frequently when you were helping others resolve a conflict?

   _____

3. To what extent are the styles you used consistent with your preferred and back-up style(s) as shown on page 18?

   _____

   _____

   _____

Learn the Basic Skills of Conflict Management

"It is not the presence of conflict that causes chaos and disaster, but the harmful and ineffective way it is managed. It is the lack of skills in managing conflict that leads to problems. When conflicts are skillfully managed, they are of value."[1]

---

[1] *Human Relations and Your Career*, David W. Johnson, Prentice-Hall, 1978, p. 247.

Managing conflict is not simple, but neither is it as difficult as most people assume. Effective conflict management depends upon certain essential contributions someone must bring to the situation.

THE ESSENTIAL ELEMENTS OF CONFLICT MANAGEMENT

1. Learn to recognize and address a conflict in its earliest stages. Develop the courage to tactfully point out you sense tension is developing, and then get all of the parties involved in identifying and solving the problems which are causing tensions. At the tension development stage the only skills needed for conflict management are problem solving skills.[2]

   At the role dilemma stage conflict management requires basic skills in communications and role clarification.[3]

2. Keep everyone focused on the conflict issues. As conflict progresses people tend to forget the issue which started the conflict in the first place. They become angry and turn away from the issue to fighting each other. Effective management requires the persons focus on the issue, and work together to resolve the issue, even while they are experiencing areas of disagreement.

3. Provide the three "P's" of conflict management:

   a. **Permission:** Give the parties permission to disagree without feeling guilty.
   b. **Potency:** Enable each one to state his/her position with strength and clarity.
   c. **Protection:** Keep each one from being needlessly hurt, and from needlessly hurting the other.

   Serious conflicts are always more quickly and effectively resolved when someone is recognized as providing the three "P's." Many times persons will subconsciously prolong the earlier stages of conflict until they feel they have the security of someone to provide them the ability to confront effectively, without running the risk of doing irreparable damage to the church or to each other.

4. Enable the parties to see a way out of the conflict situation by suggesting options to their present policies and/or behaviors. Indeed, this may be the most important function of conflict management.

   As persons become more and more involved in the conflict, their own ability to find creative solutions to their problems become narrower and narrower. It is like they are walking into a tunnel which is growing smaller and tighter—squeezing them into one pattern of thinking and acting.

   Often all of the parties sincerely want out of the tunnel, but they see no other alternative. In such instances to simply suggest a creative solution, or a satisfactory compromise, will end the conflict.

5. Work to turn every conflict into a problem to be solved—and involve all of the parties in searching for solutions to the problem. Always remember: People tend to support what they have helped to create. This is the most important principle of all.

THE THREE STEPS TO CONFLICT MANAGEMENT

After many years of working with hundreds of people in conflict, I have come to recognize that **all** conflict management depends upon three steps.[4]

1. **Generate Valid and Useful Information** about the conflict issues.

   Generating and sharing information is the first step to managing conflict. There are many ways to generate information. The process used in a particular conflict should be selected after considering such issues as: Will the parties talk face-to-face or only through an intermediary? Do they still trust each other enough to believe what they hear?

   In the companion volume to this manual, *How To Manage Conflict In The Church: Conflict Interventions and Resources*, I give concrete examples for generating and sharing information. The important thing to remember here is that:

---

[2] An excellent reference for problem solving is *Identifying and Solving Problems*, Roger Kaufman, University Associates, LaJolla, CA, 1976.

[3] An excellent reference for these is *Leader Effectiveness Training*, Thomas Gordon, Wyden Press, 1977.

[4] These three steps comprise the Chris Argyris model for changing an organization, see all of his writings, e.g., *Organizational Learning, A Theory of Action Perspective*, Chris Argyris and Donald Schon, Reading, MA: Addison-Wesley Publishing Company, 1978.

THE FIRST STEP IN CONFLICT
MANAGEMENT IS TO GENERATE
VALID INFORMATION ABOUT
THE CONFLICT SITUATION,
AND TO SHARE THAT INFORMA-
TION WITH ALL OF THE OTHER
INVOLVED PARTIES.

2. **Allow Free and Informed Choice.**

The second step is to allow the conflict parties to make free and informed choices regarding their behavior, based upon the information. This involves joint problem solving and decision making. The joint decision making involves two levels:

a. Identify the areas where there is sufficient agreement between the parties to enable them to collaborate in reaching resolutions and decisions.
b. Identify the areas where there is no agreement or room for collaboration, in order that each party may reach its own independent decisions. These decisions are then shared with the other party, and collaborative decisions are made as to how the two parties will live and work together in spite of differences.

This step can only be accomplished in a collaborative or compromising approach to the conflict. The other three approaches cannot allow everyone free and informed choice.

3. **Motivate Personal Commitment to the Agreements Which are Reached.**

Establish covenants between the parties (written or verbal) which will motivate personal commitment to carry out the agreements which are made.

Although agreements can and should be explicitly made, the personal commitment necessary to carrying out the agreements is a result of steps 1 and 2. If the first two steps are not followed, there will be little or no commitment to any agreements which may be made.

Steps 1 and 2 result in agreements to which persons are committed because they have had an active part in generating the information, in making the problem solving decisions, and they have been given the freedom to stand apart in areas of disagreement.

Step 3 is the process of turning agreements and differences into covenants (very serious promises) of support and action.

Because it is so crucial to all effective conflict management in the church, I will repeat again: PEOPLE TEND TO SUPPORT WHAT THEY HAVE HELPED TO CREATE. This method is effective because it allows the conflict parties to create the solutions to their own problems. And let me also repeat, only the collaborative and compromising approaches will allow you to follow the three-step conflict management process completely.

GUIDELINES TO EFFECTIVE CONFLICT MANAGEMENT BEHAVIOR

There are, of course, an almost infinite number of ways to actually accomplish each of the three steps to conflict management. Regardless of the methods you use your own behavior in carrying out your plan is absolutely essential to its success. Jerry Robinson and Roy Clifford have developed a set of six behavioral guidelines for collaborative conflict management. Their guidelines are listed on the following page.[5]

---

[5] Jerry W. Robinson, Jr. and Roy Clifford, *Conflict Management in Community Groups*, College of Agriculture, Cooperative Extension Service, University of Illinois at Urbana-Champaign, 1974.

Involve all parties in conflict adjustments, because people support what they help to create.

GUIDELINES	BEHAVIOR BITS

1. INITIATE DIALOGUE OBJECTIVELY
  a. Introduce subject of process to all parties.
  b. Establish ground rules for everyone.
  c. Channel communication.
	a. Friendly handshake.
	  b. "Encouraging attitude; smiling and chatting to put parties at ease.
	  c. "You both know why you are here. There's been problems over the music program, and I thought we could discuss them. Now, please tell me what is going on?"

2. INVOLVE ALL PARTIES
  a. Question, stimulate
  b. Listen actively.
  c. Accept, credibility of feelings (avoid judging).
  d. Probe for causes of feelings.
	a. Leans forward, says, "I see," "Uh, huh," and creates an open atmosphere.
	  b. Repeats and asks specific questions.
	  c. "What do you think needs to be done to solve this problem?"

3. ASSIMILATE FEELINGS AND INFORMATION
  a. Record, structure and organize ideas.
  b. Record, structure and organize facts and feelings.
  c. Record areas of agreement.
  d. Record areas of disagreement.
	a. "Is that what you mean . . . ?"
	  b. "In summary, you have said _____ and he has said _____."
	  c. "Let's list all of the ways each of you think this problem could be dealt with."

4. REINFORCE AGREEMENTS
  a. Give additional support to areas of agreement.
  b. Personalize alternative solutions in relation to benefits.
  c. Record, structure and organize agreements.
	a. "You have made an interesting list."
	  b. "Dr. Smith's research supports several of your ideas."
	  c. "Which suggestions seem most feasible? Uh, huh, I see, Do you agree? Why or why not?"

5. NEGOTIATE DIFFERENCES
  a. Affirm the right to disagree.
  b. Record, structure and organize disagreements.
  c. Identify possible compromises.
  d. Personalize alternative compromises in relation to benefits.
  e. Record, structure and organize compromise agreements.
	a. "You don't have to have full agreement on everything."
	  b. 'Let's list the major areas of disagreement."
	  c. "What would be an acceptable middle-ground position?"

6. SOLIDIFY COMMITMENT TO AGREEMENTS
  a. Review all agreements.
  b. Check for accuracy of perceptions.
  c. Confirm commitments: (1) Prepare and sign written covenant; (2) Handshake.
	a. "Let's review those points once again."
	  b. "Let's put it in writing."
	  c. "That's exactly what you should do. Go ahead."

GUIDELINES FOR THE CONFLICT MANAGER

CAN THE PASTOR OR CHURCH LEADER ACT AS CONFLICT MANAGER?

There are some situations in which a local church should call in an outside person to lead the conflict management effort. Conflicts of such seriousness are rare, however.

A skilled pastor or lay person can lead in at least 70% of all local church conflicts—and if they do, the other 30% will probably never occur.

You can lead the group in conflict management even when you are a participant in the conflict.

The approaches you may use when you are involved in the conflict or when you are outside of the conflict differ very little. The need for changes in the approach does not depend upon who is facilitating the approach, but are based on such conditions as:

1. Designs used at the tension development or role dilemma stages tend not to work as well at the injustice collecting or confrontation stages, and vice versa.

2. Designs used with small groups of persons will generally differ from those necessary with large groups.

3. Designs that work well in situations where there is moderate trust and when communications have not broken off completely will generally not work when the trust level is low and communications have broken off.

In the companion volume to this manual, *How To Manage Conflict In The Church: Conflict Interventions and Resources*, I present several concrete models for managing church conflicts. The models are all based upon the concepts presented in this step. A careful study of the models will give you many ideas for effectively managing conflicts in your own situation.

Step 3

Apply Your Learnings to Conflict Situations

You have studied your way through this volume of concepts for managing conflict and are now ready to apply them in actual conflict situations.

Let's review the essential elements of this study one more time.

ITEMS TO REMEMBER:

1. Your own conflict theology will largely dictate how you feel about conflict in the church, and what you do in response to it. Developing a sound, working conflict theology is important to becoming an effective manager of church conflict.

2. You have a style of behavior which you prefer to use in conflict situations—because this style most effectively reduces the tensions which begin to stir up inside you because of the conflict.

You probably also have another style, or two, which you fall back on if the conflict persists and your tensions become higher.

To consciously know what your style(s) is frees you to use it, or to act in a different manner. You are no longer a slave to your preferred style. You have learned a whole range of conflict behaviors from which to choose. Use this self discovery to choose your pattern of behavior, based not upon fear or tension, but upon what you believe is best in that particular situation.

3. Conflict is confusing. Emotions, words, and actions fly around erratically; colliding, stirring up a lot of dust. However, the stages through which conflict progresses are so consistent you can predict them.

Memorize every step of the conflict cycle. Begin looking at conflict situations through this model. You will soon discover you are better equipped to decide concrete steps to manage it.

4. Always work to turn conflicts into problem solving situations and to involve the conflict parties in generating information needed to solve the problems that have arisen between them.

5. This study has taught you how to head off conflicts before they get out of hand. Use your learnings to identify tensions as a signal for the need to renegotiate expectations in a straight forward manner. An ounce of prevention is worth a pound of cure . . .

6. The Christian faith provides some of the finest conflict management resources available; scripture study, prayer, preaching, liturgy, confession and forgiveness, the Sacrament of the Lord's Supper, the people's common commitment to Christ and His church. As you use these resources in a non-cohersive manner the conflicting parties will experience the peace that only God can give, and will discover the higher values which make them "one" inspite of the differences that are tending to divide them.

WHERE TO FROM HERE?

The capstone of this course is that it enables you to apply basic understandings, principles, and behaviors on conflict management to everyday conflict problems. You must now carry these learnings out of your study to the people and situations with which you work everyday.

Following are three vital steps to deepening your own self awareness and to equipping the leaders of your church to manage conflict more effectively:

1. Solicit Feedback Regarding Your Conflict Management Style From Others.

There are at least three ways to gain insight into your preferred conflict management style; one is to simply reflect on your behavior in some past conflicts and identify your prevailing patterns of behavior. A second is to use a survey to allow you to catalog your preferred responses, as you did in Section I of this study.

A third, and vitally important method, is to ask five or six persons with whom you live or work to tell you how they see you responding to conflict situations. The benefit of feedback from others is greatly enhanced when you ask them to respond by using a survey similar to the one you have used. This makes it possible for you to compare your own responses to theirs.

Your conflict management kit[1] includes a set of six forms, *How You Can Help Me Manage Conflict More Effectively: A Self-Analysis Tool*; and a form, *How To Determine Group Averages*, for use with *How You Can Help Me Manage Conflict More Effectively*. Use of the latter form will enable you to arrive at a set of group averages for comparison with your own scores on page 18 of your manual.

2. Train the Leaders in Your Church To Be Effective Conflict Managers.

Use these materials to train all the members of your ruling committees and the chairpersons of the program units.

---

[1] If you have only the Manuals, Volume 1 and 2, you may order a set of feedback forms from the publisher.

Equipping the church leaders with these concepts and tools will enable them to identify and manage conflicts before they get out of hand, the committees will learn to use conflict positively, and will become far more effective in their own ministries.

3. Utilize These Concepts and Skills Whenever You Encounter Conflict.

These tools will work to make you more effective in counseling, in conflict within your own family or social relationships, as well as in your church leadership responsibilities. In order for these tools to work for you, you must take them out of your study and into your work situation.

The companion volume to this manual, **How To Manage Conflict In The Church: Conflict Interventions and Resources**, provide several step-by-step models for managing conflicts. Study the models carefully, and use the suggested steps to plan your own approaches for managing the conflict.

THE LAST WORD

I have saved the most important word for the last: THE MOST IMPORTANT ELEMENT YOU BRING TO A CONFLICT SITUATION IS YOUR OWN SPIRIT.

Scripture declares "deep calls unto deep"; spirit communicates with spirit at the deepest level of our beings. I have found this to be especially true in my own work as a mediator in church conflict.

If your own life is experiencing unresolved conflict, the conflicts of those you are trying to help will "hook" your own conflicted spirit. Soon you will be experiencing inner tension — as though their conflict were your own. You will no longer be able to remain objective, you will be "hooked."

The most important preparation you can make in preparing to function as a conflict manager is to prepare your own spirit. For several years I have made it a point to spend a day or more in fasting and prayer as a part of my own preparation to work in a serious church conflict.

I use these hours to review my own relationships, desires and motives. When I discover conflictual desires and motives I surrender them up to God. When I discover ill feelings toward another, I write a letter or make a call confessing my feelings, asking forgiveness, etc. I pray the Psalms and ask God to assist me in the conflict situation.

I do this because I have come to realize that unless Christ shares His peace with me, I will have none to share with the people. Whenever I get in touch with the Prince of Peace I find myself filled with hope—not only for myself but for all the church. If Jesus can forgive me, show me a way out of my own conflicts, and bring His peace to my troubled spirit, surely He can do likewise with those to whom I go. You and I are the ambassadors of Christ. That means we stand in His stead in the midst of conflict to bring peace to all His people.

Mark Twain, must have known something about church conflict when he wrote, ". . . So I built a cage, and in it I put a dog and a cat. And after a little training, I got the dog and the cat to the point where they lived peaceably together. Then I introduced a pig, a goat, a kangaroo, some birds, and a monkey. And after a few adjustments, they learned to live in harmony together. So encouraged was I by such successes that I added an Irish Catholic, a Presbyterian, a Jew, a Muslim from Turkestan, and a Buddhist from China, along with a Baptist missionary that I captured on the same trip. And in a very short while there wasn't a single living thing left in the cage."

I'm far more optimistic than Mark Twain. Christians need not destroy the church because of conflict. Conflict can be managed in your church because you are there to apply the learnings you have gained in this study, mingled with a healing spirit . . .

And now, may the Peace of God
keep your hearts and minds
in Christ Jesus.
To Him who is able to keep
you from falling,
be grace and peace,
dominion and power,
both now and forever.
AMEN.

Spiritual Growth Resources

Dear Church Leader:

WANT TO LEARN MORE ABOUT MANAGING CHURCH CONFLICT?

This book is a companion volume to **How To Manage Conflict In The Church: Interventions and Resources.** This book, Volume I, has given you insights into your conflict management style, the dynamics of a conflict situation, and guidelines for managing it.

Volume II will give you step-by-step plans for actually intervening in specific conflict situations. The step-by-step plans are supplemented with selected readings and exercises in church conflict management. Volume II is a "tool kit" for your use in conflict situations.

Now that you have read volume I, you will naturally want to have volume II for your study and use in managing conflict in your own church and organization.

The two volumes may each be purchased separately, or as part of a complete study learning system, **How to Manage Conflict in the Church**. The Learning System also contains a cassette tape of lectures, worksheets to help gain further insight into your conflict management behavior, and a step-by-step study guide to lead you through all of the learning system materials.

I have also prepared a set of training designs for your use in training the leaders of your church to effectively manage conflict within their departments.

You will also want to know about **How to Manage Dysfunctional Conflict in the Church, Volume III.** It will lead you into an understanding of dysfunctional conflict situations and will give you an entirely new set of tools and approaches for working with dysfunctional persons, groups and conditions.

When the conflicts in your church seem to get worse no matter what you do, when you find yourself questioning your own leadership and counseling abilities -- the chances are you are dealing with dysfunctional conflict.

Conflicts in the church that grow out of dysfunctional relationships are different from all other types of conflict, and require entirely new tools and responses.

You may obtain all of the conflict management materials from:

SPIRITUAL GROWTH RESOURCES®

Telephone: 1•800•359•7363